MiND DELIGHTs

MARY EAKIN

HARVEST HOUSE PUBLISHERS
EUGENE, OREGON

To my kids,
Tristan and Mia,
with love

MIND DELIGHTS
Copyright © 2017 by Mary Eakin
www.maryeakin.com

Published by Harvest House Publishers
Eugene, Oregon 97402
www.harvesthousepublishers.com

ISBN 978-0-7369-7187-4 (pbk.)

Printed in the United States of America

23 24 25 / CM-CD / 10 9 8

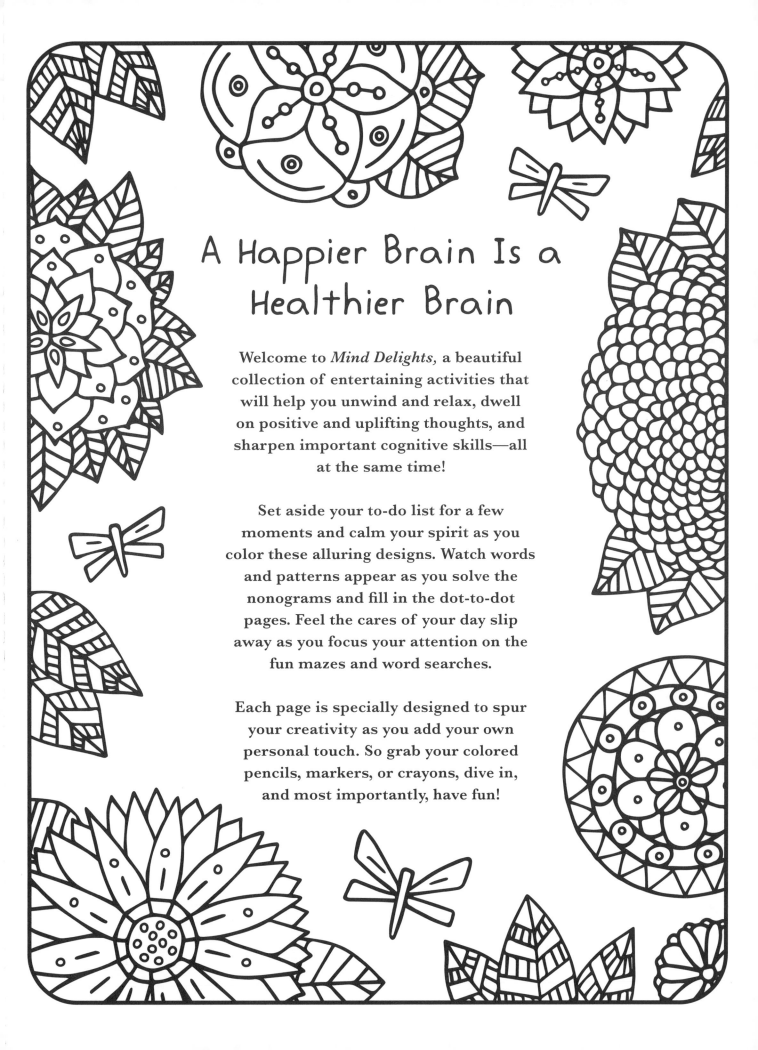

A Happier Brain Is a Healthier Brain

Welcome to *Mind Delights,* a beautiful collection of entertaining activities that will help you unwind and relax, dwell on positive and uplifting thoughts, and sharpen important cognitive skills—all at the same time!

Set aside your to-do list for a few moments and calm your spirit as you color these alluring designs. Watch words and patterns appear as you solve the nonograms and fill in the dot-to-dot pages. Feel the cares of your day slip away as you focus your attention on the fun mazes and word searches.

Each page is specially designed to spur your creativity as you add your own personal touch. So grab your colored pencils, markers, or crayons, dive in, and most importantly, have fun!

The little things

Find the words that make people smile.

```
O L S N B A L L O O N S O L S
S U S E C S E I P P U P S
S N N S N O W A N G E L S G S E
I P F R P W F P S H P H P H S H S
S M C I S M F U M U S I C I M C U
S C S O C E A N G A N E E G
E W E E K E N D S K D S W K D S
S O C E A                 O N D S N
```

God has brought me laughter. All who
hear about this will laugh with me.
GENESIS 21:6 NLT

PIE
COFFEE
PUPPIES
BALLOONS
SNOW ANGELS
SUNRISE
OCEAN
HUGS
MUSIC
WEEKENDS

Follow the good path.

1 2 3 4

Listen, my son, and be wise, and
set your heart on the right path.

PROVERBS 23:19 NIV

There are different kinds of spiritual gifts,
but the same Spirit is the source of them all.
There are different kinds of service,
but we serve the same Lord.
1 CORINTHIANS 12:4-5 NLT

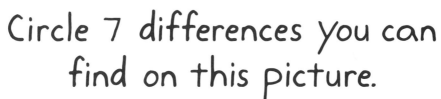

Circle 7 differences you can find on this picture.

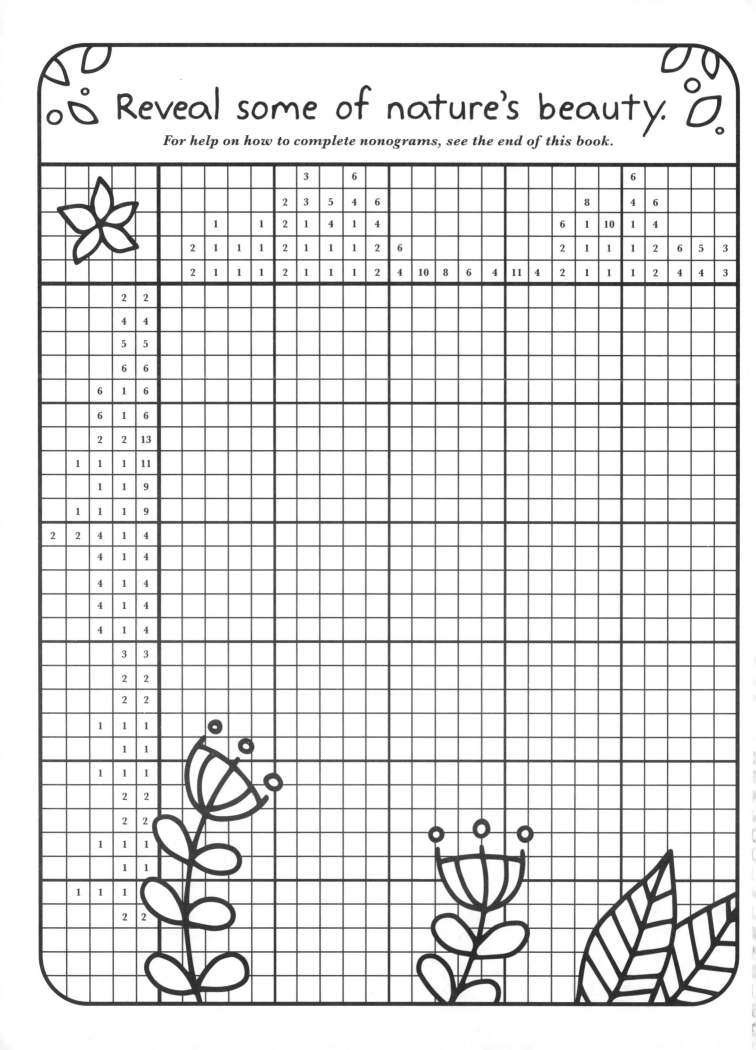

Reveal some of nature's beauty.

For help on how to complete nonograms, see the end of this book.

Get back to nature.

R G R A S S G E E R F R
S N A R J U M P I N G S
D I D F L O W E R S N J
R N F P D M F J N G R L
I N N T H G I L N U S D
B U T T E R F L I E S H
G R I A H S E R F G R E

BUTTERFLIES, UNPLUG, RUNNING,
FRESH AIR, GRASS, JUMPING,
BIRDS, SUNLIGHT, FLOWERS, FREE

For the Lord your God is bringing you
into a good land of flowing streams
and pools of water, with fountains
and springs that gush out in the
valleys and hills.

DEUTERONOMY 8:7 NLT

Find the words that make a happy home.

```
E J E                         R S G
D O O F D O O G P E A C E S N S
R N G U S T D N S T C N S R O G
E L P N U R S I R D A P D A I U
A J O Y M D R R S T W A R M T H
M R S V H Y L A U G H T E R I R
S T D C E T D C F A M I L Y D E
T Y A S M D V A V S A E Y S A S
R W E L C O M E S I G N A A R T
S T O     T N R E S A C R S T F
    E R O     O G E     S U
                        O L
```

LOVE, WARMTH, LAUGHTER, CARING, DREAMS,
GOOD FOOD, HUGS, PATIENCE, FUN, FAMILY, TRADITIONS,
WELCOME SIGN, HAVEN, RESTFUL, PEACE, JOY

Find the words that promote rest.

When you lie down,
you will not be afraid;
when you lie down,
your sleep will be sweet.
PROVERBS 3:24

```
A T B R E A T H E T
O C E L I M O M A H C S
A R O M A T H E R A P Y
S O L L A B S S E R T S
K L A W M U S I C E C E
C O M E G M A S S A G E
C S T R E T C H D O
```

AROMATHERAPY, STRESS BALL,

MASSAGE, WALK, STRETCH,

MUSIC, CHAMOMILE,

BREATHE, READ,

COLOR

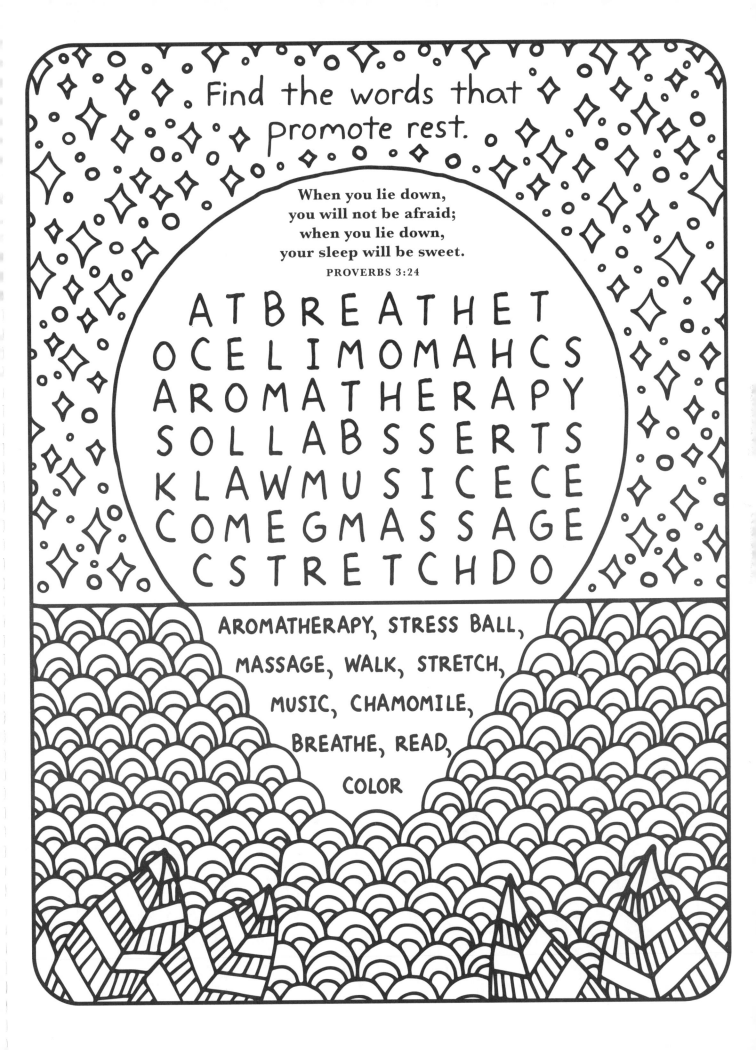

Arise, shine, for your light has come,
and the glory of the Lord has risen upon you.
ISAIAH 60:1 ESV

Circle 7 differences you can find on this picture.

Draw your favorite thing
in this world.

Soar

The wild animals honor me,
the jackals and the owls, because
I provide water in the wilderness and
streams in the wasteland, to give drink
to my people, my chosen.

ISAIAH 43:20

Find the words that help inspiration.

```
D O O D L E T L R E F L E C T E
A I C S O L C Z E S Z L S L C E
Y C S O C I A L I Z E A I E S A
D C T C Y N A R T E R U T A N T
R U R N O A R T N R U T E R O K
E N O N G N R N O A R T N M R L
A R T N A R N S N S N T R I N A
M T R Y S O M E T H I N G N E W
B R E A T H E D C M H N H D M R
H I A M E D I T A T E M G R N I
G M D T A A T E M G Y S O M E T
I R N A R N S N S N T R I N A E
E N O N G N R N O A R T N M R L
```

TRY SOMETHING NEW, DAYDREAM, SING, READ, WALK, WRITE, MEDITATE, YOGA, NATURE, BREATHE, DOODLE, REFLECT, CLEAR MIND, SOCIALIZE, DISCONNECT

Getting wisdom is the wisest thing you can do!
And whatever else you do, develop good judgment.
PROVERBS 4:7 NLT

Circle 7 differences you can find on this picture.

COMPASSION, GENEROSITY, CALM, WARMTH, HUMOR, OPTIMISM, HELPING OTHERS, LOVE, KINDNESS, SMILES, PEACE, AFFECTION

A joyful heart is good medicine,
but a crushed spirit dries up the bones.
PROVERBS 17:22 ESV

Find the words that are good
for the spirit.

ITKEWMNEROCEHFFECTKEWHECO
AFFECSPOSAFFECTIONIPAFOTR
EWHEIFRTRONLOAEHMNOWPETE
AKOSMILESEAPIWLLODCAFECO
OMTINRRHNAIOTOMTNTRATA
CEOTEOPEUENOVPENEOMES
GEPCSITYMGENEROSITY
COMPASSIONAASMSGH
WMNEROTRECIGO
OPNOHIRES
RHREESM
SARNO
S

Take care of

There's only one

Reveal some of nature's beauty.

For help on how to complete nonograms, see the end of this book.

Column clues (top, read as rows from top to bottom):

Row	Values (left → right)
1	3 · · 3 2 · · · 2 3 · · 3
2	3 2 1 · · 1 3 1 1 · · 1 1 3 1 · · 1 2 3
3	5 2 1 1 2 2 1 3 1 1 1 1 3 1 2 2 1 1 2 5
4	5 7 4 3 3 2 2 1 2 2 3 2 2 2 3 2 2 1 2 2 3 3 4 7 5
5	4 6 3 4 5 6 6 5 4 3 2 1 9 1 2 3 4 5 6 6 5 4 3 6 4

Row clues (left side, top to bottom):

			5
			7
3	3	3	3
6	2	2	6
4	3	3	4
3	1	1	3
3	1	1	3
		2	2
2	1	1	2
3	1	1	3
4	1	1	4
2	1	1	2
3	1	1	3
2	1	1	2
2	1	1	2
		3	3
		3	3
3	1	1	3
		5	5
3	1	1	3
		3	3
	1	7	1
	2	5	2
	3	1	3
	4	1	4
	4	1	4
	5	1	5
	5	1	5
	6	1	6
			13

See that no one pays back evil for evil,
but always try to do good
to each other and to all people.
1 THESSALONIANS 5:15 NLT

Circle 7 differences you can find on this picture.

Hope

Having hope will give you courage.
You will be protected and
will rest in safety.

JOB 11:18 NLT

Draw yourself
truly happy.

Let love be genuine.
Abhor what is evil; hold fast to what is good.
ROMANS 12:9 ESV

Circle 7 differences you can
find on this picture.

Find words that can improve your life.

```
R E D I S T U O T E G S
C I E D U C A T I O N O C A
M A I N T E N A N C E O E N
O P E N M I N D M I A D I M
H E A L T H Y F O O D R H F
C R E T T U L C E D L E U C
T O P T I M I S M T S I
G O R G A N I Z E T
E S I C R E X E
```

OPEN MIND,
ORGANIZE, EXERCISE,
GOOD REST, EDUCATION,
MAINTENANCE, REPAIR,
OPTIMISM, DECLUTTER,
HEALTHY FOOD,
GET OUTSIDE

Save yourself like a gazelle
from the hand of the hunter, like a bird
from the hand of the fowler.
PROVERBS 6:5 ESV

Elevate

Raise yourself to a higher level.
You can be amazing.

Reveal some of nature's beauty.

For help on how to complete nonograms, see the end of this book.

Whatever you do, do well.
For when you go to the grave,
there will be no work or planning
or knowledge or wisdom.

ECCLESIASTES 9:10 NLT

Circle 7 differences you can find on this picture.

Find the words that give people courage.

GOOD FRIENDS, BELIEVING, LOVE, TENACITY, STRENGTH, URGENCY, EMPATHY, HONOR, KNOWLEDGE, PERSEVERANCE

```
S E N M B E S
T R E I V E G
N E D V K G T
G N G O D R E L
L S O K F V N
G R O I N G S
A T E D V K G T
R G N F O I D R
V I N G R N G I E
E I V G H I G V K N
N M B E L I E V I N G
T B C P U R G E N C Y O T
A T E N A C I T Y D R N W H
G L S A Y T O N G H S L G L N
R E H L R H R C T O D R R E C
G D E O D Y V K G N I N G D N
M G R V N M B W T O R O M G I
C E P E R S E V E R A N C E Y
```

He has told you,
O man, what is good;
and what does the Lord
require of you but to
do justice, and to love
kindness, and to walk
humbly with your God?

MICAH 6:8 ESV

Don't let evil conquer you,
but conquer evil by doing good.
ROMANS 21:21 NLT

Rise above

We rejoice in our sufferings,
knowing that suffering produces endurance,
and endurance produces character,
and character produces hope.

ROMANS 5:3-4 ESV

Circle 7 differences you can find on this picture.

Find things to be thankful for.

```
O M B M R B O T D F O O R S
F O O D D E L I V E R Y O E
R D O E N I C H I L D R E N
A E K N I N E R Y E M O D I
I E S R Y G D O T C E E R Y
N R D R I A R T O T D F O O
B F I M E L C M E R I M I A
O Q F O T I M E F I C I M E
W T R B I V C M F C I Y F I
S W E E K E N D S I N S W E
S W E N R D Y S U T E I U Q
R E N H O L I D A Y S L N R
```

FOOD DELIVERY, BEING ALIVE, MEDICINE, FREEDOM, ELECTRICITY, WEEKENDS, ART, TIME, BOOKS, CHILDREN, RAINBOWS, HOLIDAYS, QUIET

Delight

**This is the day that the Lord has made;
let us rejoice and be glad in it.**

PSALM 118:24 ESV

Reveal some of nature's beauty.

For help on how to complete nonograms, see the end of this book.

Column clues (top):

Col	r1	r2	r3
1	2	2	2
2	4	4	2
3		12	2
4		13	2
5		13	2
6		12	2
7	8	3	2
8	9	3	2
9	9	2	2
10	12	3	3
11		12	16
12		11	2
13		7	2
14		7	2
15		11	16
16	12	3	3
17	9	2	2
18	9	3	2
19	8	3	2
20		12	2
21		13	2
22		13	2
23		12	2
24	4	4	2
25	2	2	2

Row clues (left):

- 4 4
- 11
- 3 13 3
- 23
- 25
- 25
- 23
- 11 9
- 11 10
- 8 3 2 8
- 6 3 2 6
- 7 2 1 7
- 6 6
- 8 8
- 3 3 3 3
- 2 2
- 1 1
- 1 1
- 1 1
- 1 1
- 1 1
- 1 1
- 1 1
- 1 1
- 1 1
- 1 1
- 2 2
- 25
- 25

wish

If you remain in me and my words remain in you, ask whatever you wish, and it will be done for you.

JOHN 15:7

Ask and it will be given to you;
seek and you will find;
knock and the door will be opened to you.

MATTHEW 7:7

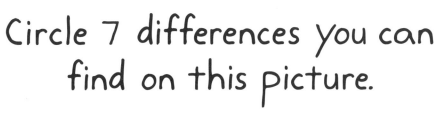

Circle 7 differences you can find on this picture.

Find the words that increase opportunity.

```
    O R R S O C I O
  A S P E E F F M I A E S
  S E K M A K E M I S T A K E S
  I N G S B D E T R Y N E B E D W
  V O L U N T E E R S O C I A L I Z E
A N C A T I O N P N E W T H P O S N P N
E O D U C A E O S E D U C A E S T C O U
S H T R Y N E W T H I N G S B N U R S G
N P N E W T H R B E S T E F F O R T
U E D U C A T I O N E K N E W T E O
O F F O R T V C R I D U C A E O
  E D U C A I O N T I O N C G
    E W T N D I N G S B
      U G O E O U
```

VOLUNTEER, GET OUTSIDE, EDUCATION, BEST EFFORT, SOCIALIZE, READ, TRY NEW THINGS, KEEP STRIVING, MAKE MISTAKES, BE KIND

Prosper

Dear friend, I pray that you
may enjoy good health
and that all may go well with you, even
as your soul is getting along well.

3 JOHN 2

Time to

Reveal some of nature's beauty.

For help on how to complete nonograms, see the end of this book.

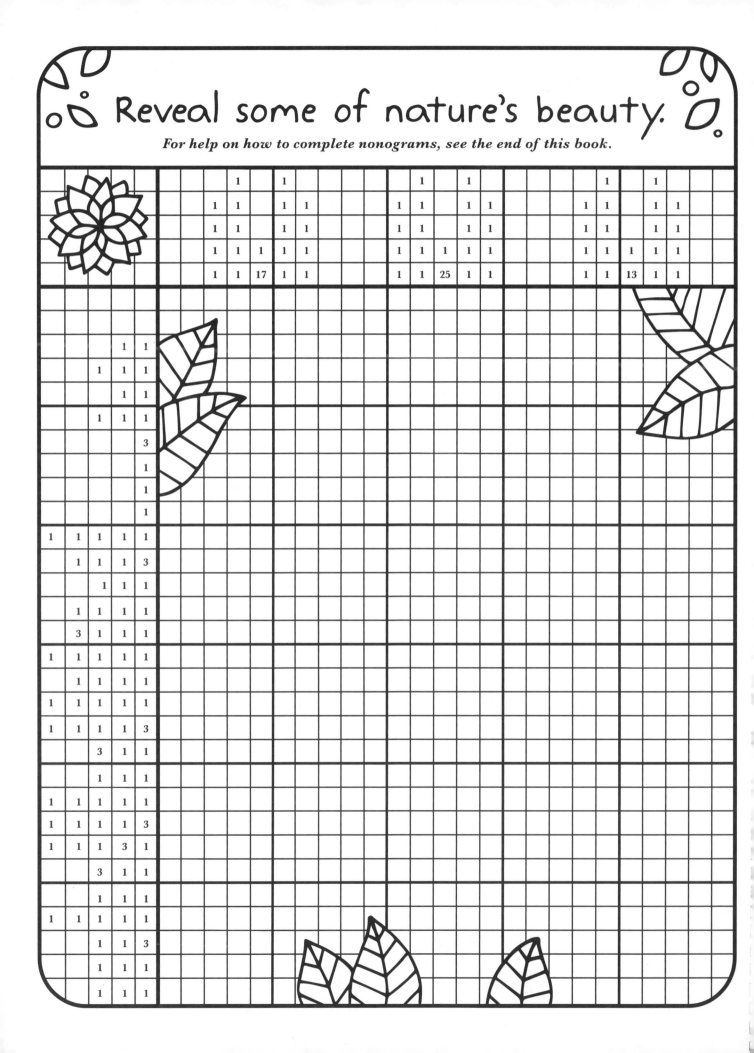

Let your light shine before others, so that they may see your good works and give glory to your Father who is in heaven.

MATTHEW 5:16 ESV

Circle 7 differences you can find on this picture.

How to solve nonograms

A nonogram is a logic puzzle that, when solved, reveals a picture. There are many ways to solve nonograms, but here are a few tips to get you started.

- The numbers on the top and left are your clues. They tell you how many boxes in a column or row need to be colored in. The order of how you place the blocks of numbers is top to bottom and left to right.

- The number blocks cannot touch each other. There could be one or several boxes between the number blocks.

- Fill in first any numbers that complete a row or column. This can help give you a clue about the rest.

- Look for any overlap. When you have a big number, wherever you put it, some of the squares will end up solid.

- Try using a dot or x to mark the spaces you know are empty.

- Never guess a box to be shaded in. One error can throw off the whole puzzle.

- Have fun!

COMPLETED NONOGRAM